PETERS MARY

HOW TO LET GO OF A TOXIC LOVER

Proven ways to heal from a toxic relationship

TABLE OF CONTENTS

Chapter 1- Realize that you merit solid love and that you're in a toxic relationship.

Chapter 2 - Recall what your identity is and find useful ways to assist you with adapting

Chapter 3- Don't expect closure and learn to be ready to forgive

Chapter 4- Encircle yourself with positivity and don't expect it to simple

Chapter 5- Get help when necessary

INTRODUCTION

By definition, a harmful relationship is a relationship portrayed by ways of behaving with respect to the poisonous accomplice that are genuinely and, not rarely, truly harming. While a solid relationship adds to our confidence and profound energy, a poisonous relationship harms confidence and channels energy. A sound relationship includes common consideration, regard, and sympathy; an interest in our accomplice's government assistance and development; and a capacity to share control and navigation. So, a solid relationship includes a common longing for one another's satisfaction. A solid relationship is a protected relationship, a relationship where we can act naturally unafraid, where we feel great and secure. A harmful relationship, then again, is definitely not a protected spot. A poisonous relationship is portrayed by uncertainty, conceit, predominance, and control. We risk our very being by remaining in such a relationship. To say a poisonous relationship is useless is, best case scenario, a misrepresentation.

Remember that it takes two people to have a harmful relationship, meaning our own words and activities matter too. At first, we'll take a gander at the ways of behaving of the poisonous accomplice, however we should look similarly hard at the person who is the recipient of the harmful way of behaving. Furthermore, we should ask, Why? For what reason does a grown-up stay in a relationship that will unavoidably harm the person in question sincerely or potentially genuinely?

How to let go of a toxic lover teaches how to:
- Admit you're in a toxic relationship
- Never forgetting your identity
- How to walk away from a toxic lover even without closure
- Getting help

And lots more……

How to let a toxic lover go will give you the tools and facilitate your walk of freedom from your toxic partner

CHAPTER 1

A contributor to the issue with leaving harmful connections is accepting that we can change the inconceivable and turn the useless "love" into a solid relationship.

On the off chance that we don't really accept that we are meriting a mindful, smart, mindful partner , we frequently draw in partners who don't accept it by the same token.

 You might feel that you do not deserve solid love due you your age, profession, weight of some deficiencies you might you have shown . You should begin to adore your self and embrace your flaws and imperfections. A partner should be fortunate to be with you. The more you accept that you deserve solid love the more you will relate to warnings or cautioning chimes and draw in a utilitarian relationship.
Encircle yourself with loved ones that are in sound and adoring connections. This will advise you that 'great love' is out there so you can increase present expectations of what you acknowledge in a relationship.

A relationship ought not be a wellspring of show and fervor: look for your rushes somewhere else. Show prompts struggle, flimsiness and unpredictable way of behaving which doesn't prompt bliss or satisfaction in any relationship.

Assuming you fear being separated from everyone else, you could tolerate conduct by your partner that could never be considered satisfactory by a companion or partner,Being separated from everyone else is much better than having your pride and dignity split the difference. Isolation is an extraordinary time for self-refection, professional success or investing energy with individuals that esteem you.
It's smarter to end something and attempt to begin a new thing than detain yourself in expecting the unthinkable. Frequently, the hardest part of a harmful relationship is breaking out of it in any case - thus a lot of this can be implanted in our family ancestry, with our choice to remain impacted by our past. Did you experience childhood in a family where hostility and unpredictable, useless way of behaving was the standard? Assuming this is the case, you are encountering what Freud called Repetition Compulsion. Your past is slipping into your present.

You acknowledge awful way of behaving as the standard since you relate to the commonality of this unsuitable way of behaving. It is critical to comprehend that you are not your previous history, you are not the way in which others have at one at once. The time has come to define clear solid limits fair and square of regard, empathy and thoughtfulness you merit.

Make it a point to leave a relationship that is damaging to your confidence and that is done serving you. Advise yourself that you are pushing ahead, away from this self-harming inclination and towards a superior, more promising time to come.

In accepting that you're in a toxic relationship It's enticing to think back on past connections, poisonous or not, with rose-colored glasses, neglecting the intricate reasons the relationship needed to end. we can really adapt to the deficiency of the relationship by completely tolerating and seeing all that was the matter with it.

Leaving any relationship, poisonous or not, makes a despondency reaction like a loss.The individual needs to go through the phases of tolerating that the relationship was harmful and that leaving was the most ideal choice. When that occurs, the individual needs to go through feelings like hurt, outrage, misfortune and pity.

Adapting in a sound manner likewise requires making re-acclimations to their life at all levels: mental changes, actual changes and natural changes. A poisonous relationship leaves individuals with flotsam and jetsam, yet when these changes occur, the adapting becomes simpler.

The dream of what could be will keep you stuck. Like clockwork. It very well may be better - such a ton better - however only not with this individual. How would you be aware? Since you've been attempting. Also, you're worn out. Also, there's something else to give.

The dream remains among you and reality and tosses blossoms at your feet so you never turn upward and see things as they are.

The more you fantasize about what could be, the more the fact of the matter is adorned and changed into something sensible. The dream will convince you to hang on for somewhat longer, and consistently at the expense of pushing ahead. Lose the dream that things will be unique. They will not be. On the off chance that you might have experienced the dream with this relationship, you would have done that at this point. Let your dream rather be one of the relative multitude of washouts who have at any point crossed your way spread on the love seat, wearing droopy Star Wars clothing as they look at your photograph, pay attention to Adele and lament like distraught truly losing you, while you eat tacos, pay attention to Beyonce and not miss them by any means. There you have it.

Love frequently has an approach to blurring your insight, which here and there makes it challenging to a recognize the truth about somebody. To escape an undesirable relationship, you should remove your affection goggles and take a gander at the individual impartially. Consider conversing with a nearby relative or companion or in any event, tracking down a specialist to assist you with taking a gander at the relationship unbiasedly.

It is entirely expected to clutch the great recollections of an ex and totally shut out the terrible recollections as it were. Keep up with your viewpoint by recalling the two sides of the experience. Help yourself to remember the great times, yet remember those terrible times or you could wind up failing to remember why you cut off the friendship in any case.

CHAPTER 2

You were an individual before you were in a harmful relationship, yet it can frequently be difficult to recall who you were before the poisonousness started to work on your healthy identity regard. Recuperating is tied in with recollecting your qualities and understanding that you truly do merit a solid relationship.

Frequently, individuals in useless connections begin to lose themselves, neglect themselves and their bliss is many times presently not a need . This can be difficult to perceive when one has put such a lot of time and exertion in a relationship. A degree of trustworthiness is should have understood and concede when a relationship has run its course as conceptualizing existence without your partner is frequently troublesome.

You nearly need to detox yourself from the convictions and values that you made together and help yourself to remember the significance of oneself .Self-empathy is critical to guaranteeing you can endure the reaction of leaving this sort of relationship. This interaction is about people getting to know themselves and their value and perceiving that what they had was not beneficial for their prosperity.

At the point serious areas of strength for when are involved, what you conclude one day can take a secondary lounge the following day. You can leave your partner and afterward wind up allowing him/her another opportunity hours after the fact. That is the major reason for finding useful ways to stop your feelings getting the better of you.

Log your sentiments on consistent schedule with the goal that you have a strong proof of how your partner causes you to feel. We frequently mistake affections for realities; we will quite often rationalize our friends and family ('however he was drained to the point that day, maybe that is the reason he took hard drugs and lashed out').
Having it written down gives undisputed proof of how you felt, how what was said or how your partner treated you hurt you, etc. Proof, proof, proof. Push it along for possibly 14 days; toward the finish of that time, investigate your considerations, activities and sentiments.

Does this individual value you? Does the person in question merit you? Does the individual in question get you enough way be dealt with? Pursuing that last choice to leave is intense, however you should put yourself first and be straightforward with yourself.

Whenever you have chosen to end it, pick a protected spot to say a final farewell to your accomplice. Harmful connections frequently include force, both profound and physical, so pick where your accomplice would be humiliated to gain out of influence.

Make an honest effort to move center off the relationship and back to yourself. Consider attempting new things or focusing on a side interest you've ignored. Recalling why the relationship was unfortunate and zeroing in on what it is you truly do need in a relationship can enable.

In particular, work on your relationship with yourself. Center around developing self esteem and regard. Advise yourself that you deserve love and that you merit a sound relationship.

In particular, work on your relationship with yourself. Center around developing confidence and regard. Advise yourself that you deserve love and that you merit a sound relationship.Letting go is difficult, and forgetting our own physical and close to home wellbeing after an excruciating breakup is entirely expected. The misery can be overpowering and we might begin to disregard our own necessities.

Help yourself by deciding to rehearse taking care of oneself consistently. Get a lot of rest. Eat nutritious food. Enjoy. Wash up. Get a back rub. Anything it is, simply effectively meet your own requirements.

Besides, practice self-sympathy. Continuing on can be a major and unnerving step, so be delicate with yourself as you mend and make another life after this relationship.

Advocate for yourself! On the off chance that you can't adore yourself, how in the world are you going to cherish another person? The equivalent can be said for removing harmful connections.

Ask yourself: What do you look for from a relationship? How would you like to feel? A sound relationship ought to be loaded up with common regard, correspondence and love. Indeed, even on the most awful day, love ought to in any case feel like love. How would you like to be cherished? Is it true that you are getting that in your relationship? In your companionships? Does it feel uneven? It could require a touch of work with a pen and paper, however invest some energy recording your sentiments about the relationship.

Then, ask yourself: Is this relationship serving me? Perhaps the relationship has changed starting from the start. Maybe you fantasize about how you wish things could be or the way that you wish things were like they used to be. While we as a whole long for the ideal relationship, in the event that this fantasy hasn't worked out as expected or it has failed into ancient history, it very well may be an ideal opportunity to rethink. A solid relationship ought to be the wellspring of bliss and energy, continually developing you to improve you, not letting you down. Assuming your considerable arrangements of needs from the above question doesn't match the relationship, almost certainly, it is done serving you and the time has come to leave.

What is keeping you down? As you've dealt with the past inquiries, wonder why are you still in the relationship. Assuming you actually have confidence in the dream, now is the right time to quit rationalizing. You have the decision in this present circumstance. Try not to sit around idly for something to change. Try not to trust that the arrangement will fix mysteriously fix itself since that won't occur. Advocate for you and what you need. The past can't direct and control your future — decide to embrace current circumstances. You want to go with the decision that is an ideal best for yourself as well as your emotional wellness.

CHAPTER 3

Quite possibly of the most ridiculously excruciating thing that accompany cutting off a poisonous friendship is the absence of conclusion - yet is the individual who caused you such a lot of agony truly going to apologize and concede their bad behaviors? I think not.

While cutting off a poisonous friendship, many individuals are searching for conclusion or a conciliatory sentiment for the aggravation or grief.

That statement of regret never comes, and individuals wind up having a more terrible outlook on things than they did when the discussion began. We have zero control over anybody yet ourselves, not make any difference the amount we might need to.

We just have control of ourselves, and our own longing for development and change. Regardless of to what lengths we will go for somebody to change, realize that they need to change their way of behaving, and no one but they can pursue the choice to make any modifications in their lives.

It harms us to see individuals be pointless, yet they should see that what they are doing isn't working, and that they need to search for choices. We could sit around idly, yet that opportunity might in all likelihood won't ever show up. This is where the idea that we want to find the conclusion in ourselves comes in.

We want to realize that we didn't merit the unfortunate treatment, and that the most ideal option for ourselves is to continue on and truly know in our souls that we merit better.

Whether you're as of now in an undesirable relationship, or you're searching for ways of recuperating from a past poisonous relationship, don't hang tight for their expression of remorse. We use immeasurably a lot of mental energy into wishing that this individual comprehended what they fouled up. As you continued looking for conclusion, it prompts disdain and further mental torment. A harmful individual won't ever apologize. All things considered, they will move the fault, wind the story, and mislead persuade you that their memory of the fact of the matter is the right one. They utilize this type of conciliatory sentiment as a substitute type of control. In any case, why even bother with a conciliatory sentiment assuming it is phony and constrained?

Pardoning is difficult. You needn't bother with a statement of regret from this individual to push ahead. However, a central stage in pushing ahead is gaining from the past. In this way, all things considered, excuse them. Absolution is a purposeful method for shutting the part on this poisonous relationship and reclaim your own power. While you can never change what occurred, you can change what happens proceeding. Your future self can't step forward assuming that you're continually being kept down.

Assuming that we've gone through months or even a long time with somebody who works on our healthy identity regard, and we've at last made the striking stride of cutting off the friendship, pardoning can appear to be a unimaginable errand. In any case, the demonstration of pardoning is a strong one that can invigorate us at troublesome times.

A ton of us imagine that we need to hold on until sensations of harmed and outrage are settled before we can pardon somebody, Be that as it may, this isn't generally so. Pardoning is really a purposeful and deliberate demonstration. A choice reestablishes imperativeness, plausibility, and honesty to your life.

Understand that you are simply angry to the degree that you have offered your own power. Eventually, to pardon somebody means to drop the obligation you feel they owe you. It is an acquiescence and arrival of the hurt that has passed between you.

The remedy to hatred is acknowledgment, With regards to making more love in our lives, we stand prepared, similar to samurai champions, to deliver all that isn't love from our souls.

  More terrible, in the event that we don't figure out how to track down the solidarity to excuse the people who have harmed us, the previous aggravation can wind up influencing our present and future connections.

What you don't recuperate from in your past will appear in your current connections and in the everyday routine you experience now. It doesn't make any difference how frequently you change your cast or your area, the story will be something very similar until you excuse.

Without absolution, the past can turn up all of a sudden, and you will rehash the set of experiences. Nonetheless, pardoning can change your past and the present by assisting you with providing it an alternate motivation. The motivation behind your life isn't to convey a complaint.
Discharge any sensations of responsibility or lament you have encompassing the relationship. Excuse yourself for anything that occurred in the past since you can never again transform it. You can push ahead and gain from it.

Excuse your previous partner too. Relinquish any disdain you have in regards to the relationship. Take a gander at your cooperate with sympathy and compassion and comprehend that all people are helpless to botches.

Pardoning is - undoubtedly - perhaps of the hardest assignment throughout everyday life. Pardoning others is more diligently than excusing yourself, yet neither come without some difficult work.

This is the kind of thing we accept everybody experiencing psychological maladjustment battles with. We blow up with ourselves for "not being ordinary" and we lash out with others for not grasping our ailment. As the maxim goes, we can't win them all. There are continuously going to be circumstances where you wish you accomplished something diversely and there's continuously going to be individuals who don't treat you the manner in which you figure you ought to be dealt with. In any case, what you do pushing ahead is altogether doing you and it begins with pardoning.

Figuring out how to continue on has a great deal to do with excusing those from an earlier time, including yourself. All things considered, continuing on can appear to be incomprehensible when you have a fabulous time and chain connected to the past.

Attempt to stress with the individual you're attempting to pardon, whether it's yourself or another person. Come at the situation from their perspective and attempt to comprehend the reason why they did or expressed the things they did. You don't need to concur with it yet attempt to figure out it. Excuse and let it go in light of the fact that you can't change what occurred yet you can change what occurs.

CHAPTER 4

It seems like a banality, yet encircling yourself with inspiration can affect your viewpoint.

It's significant while pushing ahead to fill your existence with soul advancing exercises and elective wellsprings of bliss,. Complete your life by zeroing in on the things that satisfy you - family, companions, work and leisure activities.

This is an opportunity to zero in on your assets and embrace the new life you are going to set out on. Self esteem and taking care of oneself is fundamentally important during this recuperating time. Encircle yourself with individuals who will have a brilliant, positive presence in your life. Individuals that help, care and empower what is best for you.

Remain occupied with those that you can trust and trust in. On the off chance that you are encountering a ton of disappointment, misery, disarray and outrage, this is a protected source for you.

Try not to disregard your taking care of oneself. Right now is an ideal opportunity to be a piece egotistical, as a matter of fact. In the event that you're more thoughtful, invest some calm energy with an extraordinary book. Encircle yourself with companions and friends and family who are your care group.

Make a positive climate around yourself. The best method for cleansing the harmfulness from the past relationship is to supplant it with energy. Take a walk. Take a yoga class. Write in an appreciation diary. Begin another contemplation practice or digital recording. This time ought to be centered around you and filling the cash safes of your very own health. Do what feels much better. Make yourself grin.

The best method for cleansing the harmfulness from the past relationship is to supplant it with inspiration.
Astounding things can happen when you let go.

we frequently say 'energy won't fix you however it certain as damnation will help.' Make it your objective to improve as a, more sure individual. It resembles a retribution variant of yourself; working on yourself so much and accomplishing such an extraordinary life and tossing it in your pasts' face - actually no, not others' countenances. On the off chance that you are genuinely over something, you will never again mind to cause them or it pay or to experience the anger of your wrath. Along these lines, embrace that inspiration.
Invigorate your reserve by investigating which companions or relatives can uphold you (and you, them!). Indeed, even one individual is sufficient. They will give you boldness and a thought of what life can be outside a poisonous relationship. You can likewise consider connecting with a specialist, or finding a care group.

On the off chance that you're experiencing difficulty relinquishing the past, consider engaging in a reason you have an energetic outlook on. Doing this can not just consume your time and brain as you process sentiments and let go of the relationship, however it can likewise assist with moving your concentration to an option that could be greater than yourself. Studies have shown chipping in can fundamentally work on generally prosperity. This can give point of view and assist you with feeling much better as you likewise help your local area.

These are individuals who will remain by a large number of you cut off the friendship. You'll require them for consistent reassurance, help finding a new line of work, or thoughts of another spot to live.
Similarly as breaking out of a poisonous relationship is troublesome, enduring once you're in a new, single world is hard as well - and you ought to plan for the difficulties leaving will bring.

You should figure out how to be content once more, similarly as you figured out how to adapt in the poisonous relationship,Search for bliss and satisfaction in the little things. Before you nod off every night ask yourself what three things fulfilled you today, regardless of whether it's a stroll in the park or an espresso with a companion. Accomplish a greater amount of these things.

In poisonous connections, your character can get crushed to the point that you might have not been permitted to express your genuine thoughts, or develop, or create. Venturing out again into the enormous wide world can feel overpowering to the point that you don't actually have the foggiest idea who you are any longer. You might have begun to wear a veil just to get by - and you may not actually know about the cover you have been wearing.

Try not to feel strain to hurry into anything - go at your own speed,Be thoughtful to yourself however don't turn into a survivor of what has been going on with you. All things being equal, search for what you found out about yourself, however attempt to do this from a nonpartisan spot where you can remove the feeling from it. Ask yourself 'What kindness emerge from this?' Maybe it has made you a kinder, more sympathetic individual or a harder treat who is currently much surer of herself.

Your confidence has likely taken a battering and you will be powerless prior to becoming solid in the future, so encircle yourself with individuals you trust. There will be bunches of good days and a few terrible days - yet that is OK.

Over and over again, we're centered around continuing on from a past relationship that we don't give ourselves sufficient chance to lament. A separation (whether a positive or negative relationship) periodically feels like a passing — we never again can talk or communicate with this individual in the manner that are utilized to. However, setting aside some margin to deal with the relationship completely permits you to more readily carry yourself to individual conclusion. With the cutting off of every friendship, we dive more deeply into ourselves and this reflection point is a significant piece of self-disclosure. While we frequently call it continuing on, we are genuinely pushing ahead with our new encounters and perspectives on the world. This experience helped shape you personally.

Get some margin to deal with your sentiments. Try not to feel raced to deny your sentiments and get once more into the world.

CHAPTER 5

You need to battle for the things you love and the things you have faith in, yet something or other must be you. What might you tell somebody you love who was feeling the aggravation or the deadness that you are feeling? Inside you is more boldness and strength than you will at any point require. You are a sovereign, a lord, a contender, a fighter, you are strong and lovely and everything great on the planet - and you should be cheerful. Above all, you could need to battle for it. Battle for you the manner in which you would battle for anybody you love - savagely, strongly, courageously.

The manner in which we ponder self-centeredness is broken. Childishness is tied in with perceiving what you want and giving your very best for address those issues. Some of the time there will be aftermath, yet there will likewise be aftermath by disregarding what you really want and allowing the clamor to yell you down. You matter. What you want matters. It generally has. Now and again that will mean putting yourself first on your rundown. This is much more significant assuming the main rundown has you remotely close to the top.

The initial couple of seconds, days, or weeks following a separation can appear to be weakening. As far as some might be concerned, cutting off a friendship implies a deficiency of personality, backing, and business as usual. Cutting off a friendship — even a poisonous one — can be unbelievably difficult and sincerely depleting. Nonetheless, you don't need to do it single-handedly. Know when to look for help assuming that you really want it.

On the off chance that sensations of distress, disgrace, culpability, or other pessimistic feelings endure and start influencing your regular routine after a relationship closes, consider finding a certified specialist or guide who can help you process and recognize your sentiments in a sound manner. A certified psychological well-being proficient can assist you with looking at the past relationship in a protected spot liberated from judgment while you make progress toward accomplishing a more complete identity after the relationship has finished.

Regardless of whether you feel like there is no expectation subsequent to cutting off a significant tie in your life, recollect you can recuperate and you merit a sound relationship that addresses your issues and supplements you and your bliss.